What to do
when your mom or dad says. . .
"WRITE TO GRANDMA!"

By
JOY WILT BERRY

Living Skills Press
Fallbrook, California

Distributed by:

Word, Incorporated
4800 W. Waco Drive
Waco, TX 76703

Dear Parents:

"WRITE TO GRANDMA!" Have you ever said this to your children and had them ask you, "Why?"

You could answer this question by saying, "Because I told you so!" But there really is a better answer.

This issue is a matter of etiquette. Etiquette is not just an optional part of everyday living. In situations involving relationships, etiquette is essential. It is the guideline that shows us how to act in pleasing and acceptable ways, and it tells us how to be gracious around other people. Sound etiquette is based on three very important principles:

Do unto others as you would have them do unto you. Every one of us has a deep need to be treated with kindness and respect. If we hope to receive kindness and respect from other people, we must treat them with the same. Centered in this truth is the balance between "what's good for me" and "what's good for you," a balance that is necessary for the survival and growth of any human relationship.

Beauty is as beauty does. This means that our personal beauty depends on our behavior rather than on our physical appearance. In other words, it is how we act rather than how we appear that makes us ugly or beautiful. No matter what we look like, crude behavior can make us ugly, while gracious behavior can make us beautiful in a very special way.

A thing of beauty is a joy forever! Think about it. When you are around something that is ugly, you probably feel sad and depressed. On the other hand, when you are around something that is beautiful, you probably feel inspired and happy.

It is the same way with people. Being around a person who is ugly because of crude behavior is often sad and depressing. However, being around a person who is beautiful because of gracious behavior is often inspiring and uplifting. Generally speaking, people do not want to be around a person who makes them feel depressed. Instead, they want to be around someone who makes them feel good.

If we are gracious, others will desire rather than resist our companionship. This is important as all of us are social beings.

Your children come into the world as social beings possessing specific social needs. Accompanying these needs are your children's innate abilities to get their needs met, but these abilities are undeveloped. One of your jobs as parents is to facilitate the development of these abilities. You can accomplish this by doing these things:

1. Help your children observe and evaluate their own behavior as it relates to others.

2. Bring your children into a basic understanding of the three principles mentioned above.

3. Help your children clarify social expectations.

4. Expose your children to guidelines that can enable them to meet valid social expectations.

This book can help you achieve these things. If you will use it systematically (as part of a continuing program) or as a resource (to be used whenever the need for it arises), you and your children will experience some very positive results.

With your help, your children can and will know exactly what you mean when you say, **"WRITE TO GRANDMA!"** and will be able to respond graciously.

Sincerely,

Joy Wilt Berry

4

Has your mother or father ever told you to...

WRiTE TO GRANDMA!

Whenever you are told to write a letter, do you wonder...

If any of this sounds familiar to you, you are going to **love** this book.

Because it will tell you how to write any kind of letter.

SENDING LETTERS

This is Linda Lazy.

Linda Lazy seldom writes anyone a letter because she thinks that it is too much of a bother. Linda is not very gracious.

If you want to be gracious, you will write a kind and sincere letter whenever someone—

- has written to you,
- has given you a gift,
- has entertained you,
- has lost a loved one,
- deserves to be congratulated,
- has been separated from you for some time.

You should respond as soon as possible, preferably within one week of the occasion.

The few times Linda Lazy writes letters, she is angry or upset and wants to hurt someone. Linda does not care whom she hurts. Linda is not very gracious.

To make sure that all of your letters are gracious ones, you will want to remember three things:

1. Do not send a letter that you write while you are angry or upset.

2. Do not write anything in a letter that could hurt or embarrass anyone.

3. Do not tattle or gossip in any letter that you write.

Any letter you write should be written on a clean card or sheet of paper, and it should be handwritten or neatly typed.

Your letter should have four parts to it —

- the date (telling when the letter was written),
- the greeting, such as "Dear_____" or "Hello_____," (fill in the person's name),
- the body (the message, written as though you were talking to the person),
- the ending, including words like *Sincerely* or *Yours truly,* and your name. Include your last name if you don't know the person very well.

You may also want to include your address at the top or at the end of the letter, if you are not sure that the person has it.

To make sure the letter gets to the right person, you will need to address the envelope correctly.

If you are sending a letter to—

- a boy of 13 years or less, put the word *Master* before his name,
- a girl of 13 years or less, put the word *Miss* before her name,
- a male of 14 years or more, put the title *Mr.* before his name,
- a female of 14 years or more, put the title *Ms.* before her name.

Address your envelope this way:

Whenever someone does something special for Linda Lazy, she doesn't bother to write the person a thank-you letter. Linda Lazy is not very gracious.

If you want to be gracious, you will send thank-you letters whenever people—

- have had you in their homes for one night or more,
- have given you gifts,
- have done something special for you.

Every thank-you letter should include—

- the date,
- a greeting,
- a sentence which says thank you for the specific visit/gift/special deed,
- one or two sentences explaining why you are thankful, or in what way you appreciated the visit/gift/special deed,
- an ending, including your name.

A "thank you for the visit or special deed" letter should include a description of the specific visit or deed and one or two comments about something nice that happened during the visit, or as a result of the special deed.

June 15, 1984

Dear Troy,
    Thank you for inviting me to your birthday party. I had a great time! I especially enjoyed the games and the fantastic food. It will be a party I will remember for a long time.
                    Thanks again!
                    John.

If the visit or special deed turned out to be unpleasant in any way, avoid talking about the unpleasant things and concentrate on the fact that the person was kind enough to have invited you or to have done something special for you,

October 31, 1984

Dear Mrs. Lang,
    Thank you for my visit to your home last weekend. It was kind of you to have invited me. I appreciate the effort you went to to have me stay with you.

        Thank you again,
        John Finzby

A "thank you for the gift" letter should name the gift and include one or two comments about how the gift will be used or how it will be helpful.

May 18, 1984

Dear Uncle Jake,
    Thank you for the fantastic pocketknife! It really works great. I plan to use it a lot when I go hiking and camping with my scout troop.

    Thanks again,
    John

If you do not like the gift you received, avoid saying so. Instead, be thankful that the person thought of you and spent time, energy, and money on a gift for you.

February 17, 1984

Dear Grandma,
    Thank you for the
three-piece suit. I
received it in the mail
yesterday. It was kind
of you to remember my
birthday with a gift.
I appreciate the effort
you made to get and
send me the suit.
        Thank you
        again!
        Love, John

SENDING INVITATIONS

When Linda Lazy sends an invitation to someone, she forgets to include all the important information. Linda is not very gracious.

Your invitation will be a gracious one if it includes all of this necessary information:

Who. . . is being invited

What. . . the event is

Why. . . the event is taking place

When. . . the event is taking place (the exact date, and the time it is to begin and end)

Where. . . the event is taking place (the address and telephone number of the locale)

Miscellaneous information. . . telling exactly what will be done, what to wear, and whether to bring anything.

R.S.V.P.. . . . This means "respond, if you please" or "let us know whether you will be coming."

Dear Linda,

WHO	You are invited to
WHAT	a party
WHY	in celebration of my 10ᵀᴴ birthday
WHEN	On Saturday, Oct. 7, 1984
WHERE	At 7540 Hayden, Santa Rosa, California. (707) 555-7990
MISC. INFORMATION	Dress casually and bring a bathing suit, as we will go swimming.

R.S.V.P.

Sincerely,
John Finzby

RECEIVING INVITATIONS

Whenever Linda Lazy receives an invitation, she gives it very little thought or consideration and she forgets to R.S.V.P. Linda is not very gracious.

Whenever you receive an invitation, it is important
that you R.S.V.P.

R.S.V.P. stands for RÉPONDEZ, S'IL VOUS PLAÎT. These are French words which mean *please reply.*

To R.S.V.P. means to tell the person who sent you the invitation whether you will attend the event.

You can R.S.V.P. in person.

You can R.S.V.P. by telephone.

You can R.S.V.P. in writing. A written R.S.V.P. should include—

- a thank you for being invited, and
- an acceptance (which means *yes, I will come*), or
- a refusal (which means *no, I cannot come*). A refusal should include an apology and a reason for the refusal.

If you can go to the event, your written R.S.V.P. should look something like this:

July 17, 1984

Dear Chris,
    Thanks for inviting me to your birthday party. I will be able to come and am really excited about being there.
                    your paL,
                    John Finzby

If you must write a refusal, you may want your letter to be something like this:

Dear Chris,
Thank you for inviting me to your party. Unfortunately for me, I will not be able to come as I will be away that weekend. However, I Hope that every-one has a great time.
Sincerely,
John Finzby.
I WONDER IF IT WILL BE A COSTUME PARTY? THEY COULD GO AS COWBOYS AND COWGIRLS!

The important thing to remember, when you write anything to anyone, is:

Write only those things you would want someone to write to you.

If you follow this guideline, you may be sure that your letters will be well received.

THE END of frustration over writing letters.